Soap Making for Beginners

A Beginner's Guide to Make Soaps Using
Natural Easy To Find Ingredients

Richard Walter Hart

Table of Contents

Introduction	6
Chapter 1: What is Soap	8
Soap History	8
Types of Soaps	9
Soap Industry Today	10
Chapter 2: Making the soap	12
Safety Tips	12
Safety Goggles	13
Rubber Gloves	13
Pouring pitcher	13
Safety Gear for Overhead Hazards	13
Respiratory Protection	14
Equipment Needed	14
Wooden Spoon	14
Pouring Pitcher	15
Lye Container	15
Heat Safe Container	16
Digital Scale	17
Soap Mold	17
Thermometer	18
What are soap-making ingredients?	18
Base Carrier Oils	19
Natural Additives	19
Colorants	20
Scents	21
Soap Making Techniques	21

Cold-Process Technique   22

Hot-Process Technique   24

What is the difference between the cold and hot-process
methods?   25

What is saponification?   25

Chapter 3: Recipes   26

Basic Soap   27

Ingredients: 27

Instructions: 27

Bastille Soap   30

Ingredients: 30

Instructions: 31

Castile Soap   33

Ingredients: 33

Instructions: 33

Milk Soap   35

Ingredients: 35

Instructions: 35

Aloe vera Soap   37

Ingredients: 37

Instructions: 37

Lavender Soap   39

Ingredients: 39

Instructions: 40

Shea Soap   41

Ingredients: 41

Instructions: 41

Charcoal Soap   43

Ingredients: 43

Instructions: 43

Peppermint Soap 45

Ingredients: 45

Instructions: 46

Green Tea Soap 47

Ingredients: 47

Instructions: 47

Sea Salt Soap 49

Ingredients: 49

Instructions: 49

Wine Soap 51

Ingredients: 51

Instructions: 51

Grapefruit Soap 53

Ingredients: 53

Instructions: 54

Cedarwood Soap 55

Ingredients: 55

Instructions: 56

Cinnamon Soap 57

Ingredients: 57

Instructions: 58

Chocolate Soap 59

Ingredients: 59

Instructions: 59

Champagne Soap 61

Ingredients: 61

Instructions: 61

Rosemary Soap   63

Ingredients: 63

Instructions: 63

Strawberry Soap   65

Ingredients: 65

Instructions: 66

Vanilla Extract Soap   67

Ingredients: 67

Instructions: 68

Chapter 4: Tips and Tricks   69

How to use an existing recipe, and modify it   69

How to make a recipe from scratch?   70

Understanding the science behind soap making   71

How to mix colors   72

Tips for using colorants   73

How to make your colorants: 74

To make colorants using herbs: 74

To make colorants using spices: 74

How to make swirls or other patterns in the soap?   75

How to make swirls or other patterns with a special tool   76

How to add special effects such as glitter   77

Conclusion   78

Introduction

Do you love reading soap-making guides? Are you excited to learn all the facts about natural soap making? If your answer is yes, then you will be interested to read this guide book.

This is a beginner's guidebook to soap making. It contains easy-to-understand directions. It is written in a step-by-step manner.

If you are looking for a soap-making guidebook that will help you understand the basics of soap making, then this is the best book for you. If you are a beginner, then this is the perfect book for you.

The author of this book, Richard Walter Hart, has written an excellent beginner's guide book to help you understand the basics of soap making. It is not a complete guide to soap making, but it will teach you everything you need to know about soap making.

All the materials you need to make a bar of soap can be found in your kitchen or around your house. Every recipe you will use in this book is easy to follow and contains easy-to-understand directions.

We have also included 20 recipes that you can use to make your bars of soap. These recipes are easy to follow and contain easy-to-understand directions.

After reading this book, you will discover everything to know about natural soap making. You will learn how to prepare your recipe and which ingredients to use. You will find out how to mix your lye solution as well as how to make your soap mold and what materials should be used.

Let's get started on becoming a soap-making guru and begin by reading this book.

Chapter 1: What is Soap

Our skin is made up of dead cells that build up over time. Imagine how they would feel if they were not exfoliated. It would look like the mountains you see on TV after a heavy snowfall. It's a bit rough to touch but also can trap moisture as well as dirt and grime. Our skin can do this because of the dead cells that are filled with water and oil.

The water in our skin helps keep us hydrated, while the oil is what makes it soft and healthy-looking. This combination is what makes our skin perfect for our use, but can also cause problems if we don't cleanse it properly. Since we have so much oil on our skin as well as dirt and bacteria, this can cause acne or other infections to form if we do not take care of it properly.

This is why we need soap to help cleanse our skin both inside the shower or bathtub as well as out in everyday life. Soap helps us get rid of unwanted substances that might be trapped inside our pores causing our bodies to reek from sweat when we get hot or nervous throughout the day, causing us to smell bad without even knowing it.

Because our skin can be sensitive and sometimes dry, soaps are also very important to keep our skin soft and moisturized. This is where the art of making homemade soap comes into play. Not only does it help cleanse our skin but it also helps keep it healthy and clean.

Soap History

Soap is one of the oldest industries in the world. It is estimated that soap was discovered over five thousand years ago by the ancient Babylonians, Egyptians, and Phoenicians. Soap making was a very important industry to these people and they were among the first people to produce soap on an industrial scale.

During the middle ages, soaps were produced in Europe by individual households and monasteries. Most of these soaps were made from animal fats or tallow made from animal fat.

The Industrial Revolution occurred towards the end of the 18th century and into the early 19th century, during which soap became mass-produced using new techniques and manufacturing methods designed to make it cheaper to produce.

The first industrial stage of soap production saw a massive increase in how much soap could be produced as different materials beyond animal fats could be used as a base material. Some of these materials included plant oils, vegetable oils (such as olive oil), palm oils, coconut oil, and other types of organic fats that could be readily used for making soap. The second stage saw even more ingredients being added to improve or modify various properties of the finished product such as adding colorants, perfume oils, different salts, etc.

Today there are hundreds of different types of soap being produced. Soap is made for personal hygiene, cleaning, bathing, washing, and an array of other uses. The soap market is very large and it continues to be one of the most important industrial products in the world.

Types of Soaps

Soaps are made by the chemical reaction between an acid and a base and these two ingredients can be either synthetic or natural. The most common types of soaps are:

- Liquid Soap
- Bar Soap
- Shampoo/Conditioner Bar Soap

- Toilet Bar Soap
- Oil-Based Soaps (Degreasing)
- Water-Based Soaps (Degreasing)
- Soaps made with petroleum products - vegetable oil (soybean or palm) and lye
- Soaps made with animal fats and lye (tallow)
- Soaps are made with vegetable oils and lye. (Soybean, olive, canola)

Soap manufacturers use highly processed, synthetic chemicals to make their products. When you make your soap, you have the freedom to use natural ingredients. Soaps made with natural ingredients have a pleasant fragrance and are gentle on the skin.

Soap Industry Today

The modern soap industry is a highly competitive market and many large corporations dominate the industry. The largest and most recognizable brands of soap include Dove, Ivory, Lifebuoy, Lux, Palmolive, Pears, and many others. These companies sell their soap in bulk to retailers or food dealers who in turn sell them to the consumer. These brands of soap are generally labeled as being "beauty bars" or "face bars" but the reality is that they are just general-purpose household bar soaps.

There are also many chemicals and other substances that go into these soaps that you might not want to be using on your skin and in your household. There are chemicals used in the manufacturing process, fragrances, colorants, fillers, etc... that may not be healthy for you or your family or good for the environment.

Many different types of natural ingredients can be used to replace some of these chemicals or additives in commercial soaps or can be added to commercial soaps to enhance certain properties of the finished product such as adding moisturizing properties, adding antibacterial properties, adding substances that help with eliminating acne, etc... Some of these substances include olive oil, coconut oil, hemp oil, jojoba oil, and other types of plant oils and vegetable oils. These oils can also be added along with herbs, flowers, spices, etc… to give your soap a nice fragrance.

Now, let's take a look at what is required to make soap at home.

Chapter 2: Making the soap

Soap making is a craft that has been around for ages and even today it continues to be very popular among people who love to make things by hand. This is a very simple process that can be carried out in the comfort of your own home.

The soap-making process is very simple. It involves the use of easy-to-find ingredients and a few tools that you are likely to have at home. The process can be broken down into a few steps.

Let's take a look at the process of making soap.

Safety Tips

Soap making is a relatively simple process, but it does involve some safety precautions. The most serious hazard is the presence of lye. Lye in its pure form is a highly caustic chemical that can cause severe chemical burns if it comes into contact with your skin. Lye should always be handled with care and kept out of reach of children.

Lye is also dangerous if you happen to spill it on yourself or your clothing. It will cause severe burns just as if they had been caused by hot water or very strong soap.

Another danger in soap making is the presence of heat, which can cause the formation of nitrous oxide, also known as laughing gas. Nitrous oxide is highly explosive if it comes into contact with certain organic compounds such as oils and fats. This tends to occur when you are heating fats in an open container over an open fire, so just be aware that this can happen and take appropriate safety precautions.

Here is some basic safety equipment:

Safety Goggles

Safety goggles are one of the most important pieces of safety equipment. They protect your eyes from injury from splashes and flying chemicals. If you are making soap directly over an open fire, you should wear safety goggles that can tolerate a high degree of heat. You can also buy special safety goggles that protect against nitrous oxide.

At the very least, I recommend eye protection that is rated to withstand a minimum of 100 degrees Fahrenheit (38° C). There is a picture of such goggles on the right.

Rubber Gloves

If you are making soap directly over an open fire, there is a risk that you will splash lye on yourself. Rubber gloves provide some protection against these splashes. They also prevent your skin from coming into contact with lye or with hot water if you drop something in your pot or kettle. You can also make soap without using any heat at all, so rubber gloves are not necessary for everyone. However, I find that they make handling hot liquids easier if you don't have a pouring pitcher available to use as described in the next section below.

Pouring pitcher

This is essential for people who make soap without using any heat at all and would be convenient for anyone else who makes soap directly over an open fire.

Safety Gear for Overhead Hazards

Depending on what you are doing and where you are working, you might need to protect yourself from head injuries. If you are making soap directly over an open fire, you may need to protect yourself from being burned by sparks that fall into your eyes. If you are moving around a hot liquid in a pot or kettle, you might need to protect yourself from falling soapy water.

If you are making soap directly over an open fire and sparks fly into your eyes, you could be burned, so you need to protect yourself from overhead hazards. You can protect yourself from falling sparks by wearing a hat or an apron. If you are moving around hot liquids in a pot or kettle, you can protect yourself with an apron that will prevent the falling soapy water from splashing into your face.

Respiratory Protection

If you are making soap directly over an open fire, fumes from the burning wood may cause you to choke and pass out. You can mitigate this risk by using a respirator specifically made for wood smoke. These respirators have an activated charcoal filter that will help protect you from the harmful health effects of breathing in wood smoke and burning embers. They also have a foam seal around the mouth that prevents particles from being inhaled into your mouth and throat.

Now that we've covered the basics, we can cover the equipment that you will require to make soap.

Equipment Needed

Soap making requires a few basic tools and supplies. Many of these items can be found in your kitchen or garage, but some require special equipment that you might have to purchase at a hardware store or through online suppliers.

Wooden Spoon

A wooden spoon is one of the most basic tools in soap making. You will use your spoon to stir your lye water and to mix your oils and fats during saponification.

You can use a metal spoon if you prefer, but the saponification process might cause the metal to become permanently discolored. You can also use a plastic spoon if you don't mind having it melt on you, but I recommend that you stick with wood.

Wooden spoons are inexpensive and easy to find in any kitchen or hardware store. They can be found with both long and short handles. The handle length will depend on how much space you have available in your soap-making area. If you have a large kettle, a long-handled spoon might not fit inside of it, so the short-handled variety might be more convenient for your needs.

Pouring Pitcher

If you are making soap directly over an open fire, you will need a pouring pitcher to move your lye water and your oils from the pot or kettle where they are being heated to the area where you will be mixing them. A pouring pitcher is simply a pitcher with a spout so that you can pour liquids from it without spilling. You can see an example of a pouring pitcher on the left.

You can use a regular drinking glass if you don't have a pouring pitcher at home, but I recommend that you get one if you plan to do any soap making. They are inexpensive and they make pouring easier for anyone who lacks hand strength.

Lye Container

You will need some kind of container that is safe for storing lye in it and for measuring it out when you are making soap. Lye is extremely caustic, so this container needs to be made of plastic or glass and it needs to be able to handle hot temperatures without cracking or melting. The best containers for this purpose are plastic buckets with tight-fitting lids and glass bottles with tight-fitting caps. You should not use any container that has previously contained food or drink products, as these containers may have been contaminated with bacteria or other impurities.

You can find buckets with tight-fitting lids at your local hardware store or in the paint section of a hardware store. You can also get them online. The buckets pictured on the left are available through Amazon and the jars pictured on the right are available through Vitacost.

You can find glass bottles in most grocery stores and most hardware stores, especially if you look for the kind of bottles that contain olive oil or balsamic vinegar.

Plastic buckets and glass bottles are not necessary for soap making, but they do make it easier to store your lye safely and to measure it out precisely when you need to make soap. They also make it easier to mix up solutions of lye water without having to use a long-handled spoon or a pouring pitcher to move your lye water around as you would if you were using a large pot or kettle. They also prevent you from accidentally spilling your lye water, which is dangerous because it will cause severe burns if it comes into contact with your skin.

Heat Safe Container

If you are making soap directly over an open fire, you will need a heat-safe container to mix your lye water and your oils and fats in. This container should be able to handle temperatures up to around 200° F (93° C) or above. If you are using a large pot or kettle, you can use the heat-resistant buckets that are commonly used for boiling water. If you are using a large pot or kettle on an open fire, the bucket will also need to have a handle so that you can move it easily.

If you don't have a heat-safe bucket handy, you can use any other heat-safe container with handles. You can find these at your local hardware store in the paint section or in the camping section where they keep cookware and cookware sets. I've also seen them in the kitchen section of major department stores like Wal-Mart and Target. They come in varying sizes, but they all have handles and are made of heat-resistant materials such as stainless steel or thick glass.

If your container sits directly on an open fire, it may get hot enough to melt or crack eventually, so it is best to use containers that can be replaced if this happens and not things like glass jars that cannot be replaced once they break or melt.

Digital Scale

If you want to make soap that looks like it was made in a factory, you will have to use a digital scale when you make your soap. It is necessary for saponification and it is very useful for mixing up your lye water solution and mixing up solutions of essential oils. You can find digital scales at any hardware store, but they are also available online through Amazon. These scales are not necessary, but they do make measuring ingredients much easier and more precise. They also save a lot of time because they can measure very accurately in small amounts of liquid, which means that you don't need to dirty your measuring cups every time that you measure out a small amount of liquid.

Soap Mold

If you want to make soap that looks like it was made by a professional or if you want to save money on the costs associated with purchasing bars of soap from the store, then you will need some sort of mold in which to pour your soap once it has been set up to remove the excess water from the bar or slab and give it a hard skin layer so that it won't dissolve when exposed to moisture from the air. There are many different options available for molds, so I won't go into detail about them here.

I will just say that if you plan to save your soap bar rather than using it up immediately, then you should consider investing in a soap mold. If you are making soap for the express purpose of using it for cleaning purposes, then you can make your soap without a mold and just use the bowls or pots that you used to heat your lye water with or just put the soap into some other kind of mold after it has solidified and is ready to be used.

Thermometer

You need a thermometer if you want to make soap that looks like it was made in a factory. You can use a candy thermometer or an instant-read thermometer if you are making soap directly over an open fire, but if you are using the stovetop method or an electric pot, then you will need a digital thermometer to monitor the temperature of your lye water. You can purchase digital thermometers at any hardware store or online through Amazon.

Now, let's get into the basic ingredients of natural soap making.

What are soap-making ingredients?

Soap-making ingredients are called lye or sodium hydroxide, coconut oil, castor oil, olive oil, and water. These are easily available in any kitchen. You need to make sure that all these ingredients are the purest possible because impure ingredients will affect the quality of your soap. The best way to get pure oils and water is to buy them from a reputable manufacturer or dealer who only deals with pure oils and water. If you can't find pure oils and water, then try using distilled water and also virgin coconut oil which have not been used for any other purpose before.

Base Carrier Oils

A base refers to the combination of oils used in soap making that come together as one mixture after they have been combined with lye and water. Most soaps use two or three different oils but some soaps use up to four or five different oils. The most common base used by soap makers is the three oil formula. Most recipes for this type of soap use Olive, Coconut, and Palm oil in a three-to-one ratio.

In the world of soap making, Carrier Oils are oils that are used to dilute and carry other ingredients into the suds. Most of the carrier oils sold in health food stores are vegetable-derived, but there are a few exceptions. The most popular choice for soap making is Olive Oil. Other popular choices include Coconut Oil, Palm Oil, and Grapeseed Oil.

Olive oil is an excellent choice for soap making because it is inexpensive and readily available. It produces a creamy lather and leaves your skin feeling soft and silky. Olive oil has a low saponification value, which means that it reacts slowly with lye to make soap, so you have plenty of time to work with the mixture before it begins to thicken and harden. This allows you to blend your ingredients thoroughly without creating air bubbles or pockets in your soap mixture.

Natural Additives

A natural additive is an additive that is derived from a natural source. They are often used in soap making for their unique fragrance and color qualities. Natural additives can be used in place of artificial additives, but they are not always suitable for this purpose. Natural additives may contain oils or other ingredients that may lessen the quality of your final product.

Natural Additives are used in soap making to add color or fragrance to the final product. These ingredients can be purchased at most health food stores and many natural food stores. They can also be purchased online from craft supply companies. Natural additives have a wide variety of applications, but they should not be used as a replacement for synthetic ingredients.

Some of the more popular natural additives include Cocoa Powder, Ground Coffee, Cornstarch, Dried Herbs, and Powdered Milk. Cocoa powder is an excellent additive for soap making because it has a mild chocolate scent that blends well with other fragrances.

Colorants

Colorants are used in soap making to give your soap a unique look and a rich, appealing color. Colorants can help you create unique soaps that are both appealing and practical. Natural colorants are derived from plant or animal sources. They are often used in soap making to increase the aesthetic value of the final product. Natural colorants are usually more expensive than synthetic colorants, but they are also more vibrant.

The most popular natural colorant is Annatto Seed Powder. It is derived from the seeds of a tropical tree that grows in Central and South America. Annatto seed powder has a golden brown hue that can be used in cold process soap making to give your soap a beautiful yellowish-orange color. It can also be used in hot process soap making to give your soap an orange tint.

Other popular natural colorants include Titanium Dioxide, Iron Oxide (Red), and Iron Oxide (Yellow). Titanium dioxide is often used in cold process soaps because it adds a white glow to the final product without altering its pH balance. It can also be used as a substitute for titanium dioxide, which is a synthetic additive that can irritate sensitive skin types. Iron oxide (red) is another popular natural additive that can be used as an alternative for other synthetic additives like Ultramarine Blue or Red #30 Lake Pigment. Iron oxide (yellow) is often used in cold process soaps made with coffee or cocoa powder because it gives the final product a rich golden hue.

Scents

The scent is a substance that gives off fragrance to the sense of smell. The scent is often used in soap making to give your soap a unique scent that will make it stand out from other soaps on the market. Scent can also be used to reduce chemicals in additives like colorants and fragrances, which are traditionally made with synthetic ingredients.

In most cases, scents cannot be used as a direct replacement for synthetic additives because they have not been proven to be safe for this purpose. Synthetic fragrance oils are usually mixed with other chemicals and contain preservatives and artificial dyes. Natural scents are more expensive than synthetic scents, but they are also safer for use on the skin and in the home. Natural scents are available from soap-making supply companies that sell high-quality products made from natural ingredients.

Soap Making Techniques

Soap making is a very simple process and it doesn't require any kind of special equipment or skills. However, you need to be very careful while working with lye. If you use the wrong kind of containers and utensils the lye may react with them and cause injury.

There are two main techniques of soap making. The first one is the cold-process method in which you mix the lye with other ingredients and then let it sit for a few weeks to harden. The second one is the hot process method in which you mix the lye with other ingredients and then cook it to make it solidify.

Cold-Process Technique

The cold-process method is the easiest one to use. You need to mix water and lye to make a liquid solution of lye and water. The solution should be clear and not have any particles floating in it. It should not be a yellowish color or have any oily-looking surface.

Step 1: Make sure that you have all the required ingredients ready before you start making the lye solution. You will need to have a water source handy and a large container to mix the lye in. The container should be large enough to hold about 50% more than the amount of water in it. You should also have a scale to measure out all of the ingredients and containers that are suitable for storing the lye solution in them.

Step 2: Once you are ready to start mixing up your lye solution you should wear gloves and eye protection as well as a long-sleeved shirt and pants because there is a chance of some splashing while you are mixing it up. Also, make sure that there are no pets or other living things around where you will be working.

Step 3: Pour two cups of water into your container and then add one cup of lye into it. Mix these two ingredients very carefully until they are completely combined because if any undissolved chunks of lye remain they can cause injury later on when the mixture becomes hot enough to react with them. You can mix this lye solution using a whisk or even an electric mixer if you want but take care not to splash it out of the container.

Step 4: Once you have the lye and water mixed you need to add another cup of water to it. You will then add a whole bunch of different ingredients to the solution one at a time. The first ingredient is going to be the fats and oils that you are using in your soap making. You should use anywhere between 1/2 and 1 pound of fats per pound of lye solution that you have. The next ingredient is going to be the scented oils and essential oils that you want to add in for fragrance. You can use anywhere between 2 and 5 ounces for every pound of fat that you are using depending on how strong smelling you want your soap to be. Then add 3 tablespoons of a natural thickener into the solution such as clay or aloe vera gel or even oatmeal if that's what you prefer to use. Then add 1 teaspoon of light liquid oil into your mixture and after that stir in 2 tablespoons of some kind of binders, such as honey, glycerin, or even corn syrup into the solution before mixing in 4 tablespoons of an emulsifying agent such as vegetable oil, soybean oil or even any kind of light oil that you already have on hand like grapeseed oil or sunflower oil.

Step 5: Now you can add in any colorants, skin-soothing oils, and any other additives that you want to use but make sure that you are not using any of the ingredients that will cause reactions with the lye. Also, make sure to put your container somewhere safe where it won't get knocked over because there is a chance of some splashing while you are mixing everything up. Then when you are finished adding all of the ingredients into the solution slowly stir it for a few minutes to mix up all of the ingredients thoroughly before leaving it alone for a few hours so that all of the lye can react with all of the fats and oils in your mixture.

Step 6: Once your lye reaction has been sitting for a few hours then it's time to test it to see if it is ready or if you need to continue cooking it. You can do this by putting some cold water into a glass and then adding some soap shavings from your mixture into this water. If they dissolve completely within about 20 seconds, then your soap is ready to be used but if they don't dissolve completely you need to continue cooking it.

Step 7: If your soap mixture is ready to use you can pour it into the containers that you are going to use for storing it in and leave it for a few days until it hardens up. Then after that, you can use the soap and enjoy the lathering, moisturizing and exfoliating benefits of your homemade soap!

Hot-Process Technique

The hot-process method is a little bit more difficult than the cold-process method but it's still not too hard to do. First, you mix water and lye and then you cook this mixture until all of the ingredients have melted and mixed. Then you can add in any additives that you want to use and continue to cook the mixture until it has reached around 240 degrees Fahrenheit. After that, you can let the soap cool down and harden up before using it.

Step 1: Once again make sure that you are wearing gloves, eye protection, long sleeve clothing, and something on your feet that will protect them from any splashing because there is a chance of some splashing while mixing these ingredients. You should also have all of your ingredients ready before getting started with this process. You will need to have a large container, measuring cups, measuring spoons, an accurate scale so that you can measure out everything accurately, containers for storing your soap in once it has been made and any additives that you want to use.

Step 2: Pour two cups of water into your container before adding one cup of lye into it. You can then use a whisk or a hand mixer to make sure that they are mixed thoroughly and evenly. You should also make sure that this mixture is cooled off before adding in any fats or oils because if you add them while the mixture is still hot there is a chance of it getting too hot and splashing.

Step 3: Now add all of your fats and oil into the mixture one at a time while stirring them in with either a spatula, whisk, or electric mixer. The next step is to add in all of your scented oils, natural thickeners, and any other additives that you want to use into the mixture before continuing cooking it. You will want to cook this mixture for about an hour but if you don't have access to a kitchen thermometer then you can tell when it has reached the right temperature by dropping some soap shavings into cold water. If they dissolve completely within about 20 seconds, then your soap is ready for use but if they don't dissolve then keep cooking it until they do.

Step 4: Once your soap has reached the right temperature you can pour it into containers for storing it in and let it harden up before using. You will need to let it sit for a few days before using it to allow it to harden up completely. Then you should be able to use this homemade soap and enjoy all of the benefits that come with using it.

What is the difference between the cold and hot-process methods?

The main difference between the cold and hot process methods is that the former one is a little safer than the latter one. In both methods, you need to be very careful with lye. The cold process method is a little safer because in this method you only use the lye mixture for the saponification process but in the hot-process method, you also use the lye mixture for cooking which may cause injury if not handled properly.

What is saponification?

Saponification is a chemical reaction that takes place when lye interacts with oils and water. The end product of this reaction is soap.

Chapter 3: Recipes

This is the most exciting chapter, where you will be able to find many recipes for making different types of handmade soap. All of these recipes are just a few simple steps away from you. I will provide you with the basic ingredients required for making the soaps, and then you will be able to alter it as per your interest and choice.

For the recipes below, we are assuming that you want to make a single bar of soap. However, if you want to make 10 or 20 bars at the same time, just multiply the ingredients by the number of bars you wish to make.

Each bar of soap weighs approximately 4 ounces (113.4 grams).

Basic Soap

The basic soap recipe is quite simple. It uses 100% pure olive oil. Apart from that, we need a lye solution and a few other ingredients.

Ingredients:

1. Olive oil (100%) – 11 ounces (312 grams)
2. Lye – 1 ounce (28 grams)
3. Water – 4 ounces (113.4 grams)
4. Fragrance Oil – 1 teaspoon (5 ml) – Optional
5. Colorant – 1/8 teaspoon (.6 ml) – Optional

Instructions:

Step 1: Prepare the lye solution in a glass measuring cup. Put 1 ounce (28 grams) of lye into 4 ounces (113.4 grams) of water in a glass measuring cup and stir until the lye dissolves. Set it aside, do not touch it until it cools down. When the lye solution cools to below 100°F, then the temperature is safe for handling and you can mix it with other ingredients without burning your hands.

Step 2: Add the olive oil to a stainless steel pot. Make sure that the pot has a pouring spout or handle so that you can easily pour out all of its contents later on. Place it on low heat and warm up the oil until it reaches approximately 100°F-110°F (35-43°C) and then remove it from heat immediately before any soap gets cooked! The soap will continue to heat up after you have removed it from heat, because of its reaction with air and other oils present in the soap. Therefore, we need to keep it under 110°F at all times throughout this process!

Step 3: Add one ounce (28 grams) of lye solution to 4 ounces (113.4 grams) of olive oil. It is very important to add the lye solution to the olive oil under absolutely no circumstances must the two liquids mix in a bowl or container and then be poured into the pot. If it is done that way, you will end up with a soap that does not saponify properly.

Step 4: Using a hand blender, mix the two liquids until they are completely combined into one mixture. Keep mixing for at least 3 minutes after all of the lye has been combined with olive oil. We need to ensure that all of the lye has been mixed with olive oil so that we can avoid any partial saponification later on.

Step 5: Place your soap mixture in a crockpot or on low heat on an electric stove and cook it until it reaches approximately 170°F (77°C). The soap will continue to heat up after you have removed it from heat, because of its reaction with air and other oils present in the soap. Therefore, we need to keep it under 170°F at all times throughout this process! The cooking time depends upon how much water is used in each batch of soap making. For instance, if you use a crockpot, it will take approximately 1 hour for the soap to cook.

Step 6: Let the soap cool down to approximately 140°F (60°C) before adding any other ingredients. If you pour the fragrances and colorants in before the soap has cooled down, they will evaporate during the cooking process.

Step 7: Add any fragrance or essential oil that you wish to use for your soap. This can be done at any stage of the process, but it is best to add them when this step is completed so that they are well and truly mixed with all of the other ingredients. Essential oils tend to evaporate quickly, so we need to ensure that they are well mixed with all of the other ingredients for them not to evaporate during cooking! If you have chosen a fragrance oil instead of essential oil, it can be added at this stage as well.

Step 8: Add your colorant into your mixture and mix thoroughly until it is evenly distributed throughout your mixture. I use 1/8 teaspoon (.6 ml) of a lye solution, pipetted out with an eyedropper, for coloring my soap. You can also use liquid soap coloring for your soap.

Step 9: Pour your soap into a well-greased mold. If you do not have a soap mold, you can use any regular kitchen container that has straight sides and a pouring spout.

Step 10: Let your soap sit undisturbed in the mold for 24 to 48 hours. Remember, the longer the soap sits in the mold undisturbed, the harder and more durable it will become! After 24 hours, it is time to unmold your soap. I usually let mine sit for 48 hours so that they can harden up as much as possible. If you are using a plastic container as a mold, gently remove one corner of the plastic so that you can easily pull out your finished bar of soap from its mold. You can also leave it in its plastic container until it is completely dry and then cut it out of its mold once it has been dried! It is better to wait until completely dry before wrapping or cutting out your bars of soap because if left in its plastic container while still wet, they will stick to it and be very difficult to remove later on!

Bastille Soap

Here is a soap recipe that I made with some friends of mine at Bastille Day!

This soap recipe is for 100% olive oil soap with olive oil and lard base. There are no added oils or fats in this soap recipe. This soap recipe uses the cold process method of making soap, so you will need to allow time for it to cure.

Ingredients:

- Lard – 24 ounces (680 grams)
- Olive Oil – 15 ounces (425 grams)
- Lye – 2 ounces (56 grams)
- Water – 4 ounces (113.4 grams) x2 = 8 ounces (226.8 grams) total water used in this process.

You can use up to 16 ounces (454 grams) of water if you prefer a softer bar of soap that produces less suds, though there is no need to use more than 8 ounces if you are using the olive oil and lye solution method!

Instructions:

Step 1: Prepare the lye solution in a glass measuring cup. Put 2 ounces (56 grams) of lye into 8 ounces (226.8 grams) of water in a glass measuring cup and stir until the lye dissolves. Set it aside, do not touch it until it cools down. When the lye solution cools to below 100°F, then the temperature is safe for handling and you can mix it with other ingredients without burning your hands.

Step 2: Add the lard to a stainless steel pot. Make sure that the pot has a pouring spout or handle so that you can easily pour out all of its contents later on. Place it on low heat and warm up the lard until it reaches approximately 100°F-110°F (35-43°C) and then remove it from heat immediately before any soap gets cooked! The soap will continue to heat up after you have removed it from heat, because of its reaction with air and other oils present in the soap. Therefore, we need to keep it under 110°F at all times throughout this process!

Step 3: Add two ounces (56 grams) of lye solution to 24 ounces (680 grams) of lard. It is very important to add the lye solution to the lard under absolutely no circumstances must the two liquids mix in a bowl or container and then be poured into the pot. If it is done that way, you will end up with a soap that does not saponify properly.

Step 4: Using a hand blender, mix the two liquids until they are completely combined into one mixture. Keep mixing for at least 3 minutes after all of the lye has been combined with lard. We need to ensure that all of the lye has been mixed with olive oil so that we can avoid any partial saponification later on.

Step 5: Place your soap mixture in a crockpot or on low heat on an electric stove and cook it until it reaches approximately 170°F (77°C). The soap will continue to heat up after you have removed it from heat, because of its reaction with air and other oils present in the soap. Therefore, we need to keep it under 170°F at all times throughout this process! The cooking time depends upon how much water is used in each batch of soap making. For instance, if you use more water, then it will take longer to cook.

Step 6: Once your soap has reached 170°F (77°C), let it cool down and then pour the mixture into silicone molds. You can also pour your soap into a glass container and let it harden in the refrigerator. The last step is to cut your soap into bars and allow them to cure for 4 weeks or more.

Castile Soap

This soap recipe is for 100% olive oil soap with a castile soap base. It is a very simple recipe to follow and very easy to make. The only extra things you will need are some containers to pour the soap in when it is finished and some cheesecloth.

Ingredients:

Olive Oil – 14 ounces (400 grams)
Water – 7 ounces (200 grams)
Lye – 1.5 ounces (45 grams)
Essential Oil – optional

Instructions:

Step 1: Weigh the olive oil, water, and lye into a heat-proof glass bowl. Place the bowl in the sink and fill it with enough cold water to create a double boiler effect.

Step 2: Heat the mixture until it reaches approximately 100 degrees Celsius. Be very careful not to exceed 100 degrees as this will start to cook the soap. Remove from heat and allow to cool until the temperature is less than 80 degrees.

Step 3: Add essential oils if you are using them; stir well. Pour into containers and cover with cheesecloth secured with a rubber band. (This helps prevent any splashing when you pour.) Allow setting for 48 hours.

Step 4: Remove cheesecloth and cut into bars.

Milk Soap

Milk soaps are very popular. This recipe is for a castile soap base, but you can easily use this same recipe for a cold process soap. If you are using this recipe for the cold process, the lye and water will still need to be at room temperature before you add them to the olive oil.

Ingredients:

Water – 7 ounces (200 grams)
Milk – 1 quart (1 liter)
Olive Oil – 4 pounds (1.8 kilograms)
Lye – 2 ounces (57 grams)
Fragrance/Essential Oils – 1.5 ounces (42 grams)

Instructions:

Step 1: Measure the water into a large stainless steel pot. Make sure that it is at least 4 inches (10 cm) off the heat. Mix the lye and water. Finish mixing by hand until your mixture is clear. Set the water/lye mixture aside.

Step 2: Measure the milk into a stainless steel pot. Heat the milk on medium-low heat for about 5 minutes, just until it is warm to the touch.

Step 3: Slowly add the lye/water mixture to the olive oil. Mix well for 1 minute.

Step 4: Add the warm milk to your soap. Mix well and continue to mix until trace is reached (about 10–15 minutes). If you use a stick blender during this process, make sure that you keep it submerged in your soap mixture so that it does not become electrically charged by static electricity. You can test for trace by dribbling a small amount of soap onto some paper or into a bowl of cold water and seeing if it leaves a trace behind when you run your finger through it. When your soap has reached trace, add your fragrance/essential oils and mix them in well with either an immersion blender or by hand with a spoon or whisk. You can also add any other additives such as dried herbs at this time as well if desired.

Step 5: Pour your soap into molds and allow it to cure for 4–6 weeks before using (depending on how thick you would like your bars to be).

Aloe vera Soap

Aloe vera is a popular plant to use for soap. It is inexpensive and easy to grow and it produces a lot of soap. This recipe can be used as a castile soap base or you can use it for cold process soap.

Ingredients:

Water – 8 ounces (250 grams)
Aloe Vera – 1 plant (about 3–4 feet [100–120 cm] long)
Lye – 2 ounces (57 grams)
Witch Hazel (optional) – 2 ounces (57 grams)
Olive Oil – 5 pounds (2.25 kilograms)
Fragrance/Essential Oils – 1.5 ounces (42 grams)

Instructions:

Step 1: Cut the aloe vera leaves from the plant and remove them from the center. The best way to do this is to cut the leaves into smaller pieces and then use your hands to remove each of the small pieces of leaf from its center. This can be a bit messy, so if you have rubber gloves, it would be helpful. Make certain that you get all of the gel from each leaf or it will be difficult to get a good lather when using your soap.

Step 2: Mix all ingredients except for essential oils in a stainless steel pot. (The small amount of witch hazel will add some lather to your soap when you use it.)

Step 3: Heat your mixture on medium-low heat until all ingredients are melted and mixed well (about 5–6 minutes). The water/lye mixture should be at room temperature before it is added to your olive oil/aloe vera mixture.

Step 4: Add essential oils, mix well, and pour into molds.

Step 5: Allow curing for 4–6 weeks before using your soap.

Lavender Soap

Lavender has been used for centuries for its healing and soothing properties. It is a very popular fragrance in soaps and lotions. This recipe uses gentle lye, and the soap is left unscented. If you'd like a stronger lavender fragrance, add 1/2 ounce (14 grams) of lavender essential oil to your soap instead of the 2 ounces (57 grams) of fragrance/essential oils called for in the recipe.

Ingredients:

Water – 7 ounces (200 grams)
Olive Oil – 4 pounds (1.8 kilograms)
Lye – 2 ounces (57 grams)
Lavender Buds – 3 tablespoons (28 grams)
Oatmeal – 3 tablespoons (30 grams)
Rosemary Essential Oil or Rosemary Infused Oil – 1 teaspoon

Instructions:

Step 1: Weigh out your ingredients.

Step 2: In a medium-sized pot, heat the water until it reaches 100°F (37°C). Add the soap-making oil to the water and stir until it melts. Remove from heat and allow to cool to 100°F (38°C).

Step 3: While the soap is cooling, weigh out your herbs and oatmeal. Place in a bowl or on a cookie sheet and bake at 150°F (66°C) for 10 minutes. Oatmeal can be toasted in an oven at 350°F (177°C) for 30 minutes.

Step 4: Once the soap mixture has reached 100°F (38°C), add the lye and stir until dissolved. Set aside to cool to 90°F (32°C).

Step 5: Once the soap has cooled down, measure out 2 ounces (57 grams) of lavender buds and grind them into a fine powder using a mortar and pestle. Add this powder to the soap mixture, along with 1 teaspoon of your essential oil or infused oil. Stir until fully incorporated.

Step 6: Spoon batter into molds and let sit for 24 hours. Turn out onto a wire rack to air dry for another 24 hours before use. Your soap will be ready after 48 hours of air-drying time.

Shea Soap

Shea butter is a great addition to soap and lotion recipes. It helps to soften the skin and it also contains vitamins A, E, D, and F which are great for your skin.

Ingredients:

Water – 7 ounces (200 grams)
Lye – 4.4 ounces (125 grams)
Olive Oil – 8 ounces (250 grams)
Shea Butter – 2.3 ounces (65 grams)

Instructions:

Step 1: Melt shea butter. This can be done by placing the butter in a glass measuring cup and placing that cup in a saucepan with some water in it. The water should come up to the same level as the butter. The butter will melt when it is placed over the warm water but you want to make sure it does not boil.

Step 2: Mix lye with water (wear protective gloves). Make sure they are thoroughly mixed, then add to the oils and mix until trace is achieved (about 10 minutes of mixing). If you are using a stick blender, then this should happen at about 40 seconds.

Step 3: Mix shea butter with trace. The shea butter and the oils must be the same temperature because if they are not then you will get a "separation" (the shea butter will float to the top and could burn).

Step 4: Pour soap into molds, wait 24 hours and remove from molds. You can lightly spray the soap with rubbing alcohol to help release it from the mold.

Charcoal Soap

This soap is great for oily skin and it can also help to remove stains from clothing.

Ingredients:

Water – 7 ounces (200 grams)
Lye – 4.4 ounces (125 grams)
Lemongrass Essential Oil – 4.4 ounces (125 grams)
Charcoal Powder – 1/2 cup (approx. 60 grams)
Olive Oil – 1.8 ounces (50 grams)
Coconut Oil – 1.8 ounces (50 grams)

Instructions:

Step 1: The first step is to weigh the water, lye, and essential oils on a digital scale. Mix these and then allow the mixture to cool.

Step 2: Once the solution is cool, weigh the coconut and olive oils and then mix them in a separate bowl.

Step 3: Now weigh the charcoal powder and add this to the oil mixture. Mix thoroughly.

Step 4: Next, add the oil mixture to the lye solution. Stir/shake vigorously for about 5 minutes. This will ensure that all of the ingredients are well combined and create a smooth paste.

Step 5: Put on some rubber gloves and then add 1/4 cup of distilled water to the soap mixture. Stir gently with a spoon or spatula until you have a smooth paste again. Then remove your gloves and allow this paste to cool for about an hour (it should be cool enough so that you can touch it without burning yourself).

Step 6: While you wait, line your molds with some cling wrap or baking paper (this will make it easier to get your soap out of the mold once it has been set).

Step 7: Once your soap has cooled down enough, pour it into your molds. Leave them in a safe place where they can remain undisturbed until they have completely set (it usually takes 24–48 hours). Then simply take off the cling wrap and voila – you will have some lovely charcoal soap.

Peppermint Soap

Peppermint soap is great for tired or itching skin and it also has a lovely smell.

Ingredients:

Water – 7 ounces (200 grams)
Lye – 3.5 ounces (100 grams)
Coconut Oil – 7 ounces (200 grams)
Safflower Oil – 7 ounces (200 grams)
Olive Oil – 3.5 ounces (100 grams)
Peppermint Essential oil

Coloring if desired.

Instructions:

Step 1: Add the lye to the water and stir until it dissolves. Don't inhale the fumes from this mixture as it can be dangerous

Step 2: In a separate container add the olive oil

Step 3: Add the coconut oil and safflower oil to a large measuring jug or heatproof bowl.

Step 4: Add the lye/water mixture to the oils. Stir occasionally and watch out for any splashing. Don't use an electric whisk as this can create static electricity which can cause an explosion. Stir until it thickens slightly and it will turn transparent. This will take about 15 minutes, but check after 10 minutes

Step 5: Now you need to add your coloring if desired and stir it in thoroughly. Leave for another 25 minutes to an hour at room temperature until it thickens even more and will set when you tip the mixture out of your jug or bowl without running off the sides. If desired now is the time to add any extras such as essential oils or scented oils, but you can also do this at the end if you prefer (see below). Leave aside for 5 minutes before you start pouring into your molds

Step 6: The soap is now ready to be cut into bars, although if you leave longer than an hour it may be too hard to cut into bars without cracking so test a small piece first.

Green Tea Soap

Green tea has many benefits such as reducing stress and even preventing bacterial growth. This soap is great for your skin and is the soap of choice in many hotels and spas.

Ingredients:

Water – 7 ounces (200 grams)
Lye – 1.5 ounces (42 grams)
Coconut Oil – .5 ounces (14 grams)
Palm Oil – .5 ounces (14 grams)
Castor Oil – .3 ounces (10 grams)
Green Tea Extract – 10 ml
Essential Oils – 2 drops (optional)

Instructions:

Step 1: Gather your supplies including a place for the lye and water to cool.

Step 2: Weigh out the lye.

Step 3: Place the lye container in a pan of ice water. Do not put it in the water yet. This will help to reduce any chance of an explosion. Use rubber gloves, eye protection, and other safety precautions when working with lye.

Step 4: Weigh out your ingredients and add them to a non-aluminum bowl or pot (never use aluminum). The container must be made of food-grade plastic, glass, or stainless steel. The coconut oil needs to be melted so that will need to be done before mixing with the other ingredients.

Step 5: Place the bowl or pot that contains the lye and water on your scale and tare it. Weigh out the lye and water. Pour the lye into your oils without tipping or disturbing the container. Slowly stir with a rubber spatula until you have a smooth mixture.

Step 6: Use a stick blender to mix for about a minute. Keep in mind that you want to keep the soap light green in color!

Step 7: Pour into molds and allow to cure for at least 24 hours before removing from molds. If you are using essential oils, add them now and mix well.

Sea Salt Soap

Sea salt is great for exfoliating the skin and leaving it feeling soft and smooth.

Ingredients:

Water – 4 ounces (113 grams)
Lye – 1.5 ounces (42 grams)
Coconut Oil – 0.5 ounces (14 grams)
Sea Salt – 0.5 ounces (14 grams)

Instructions:

Step 1: Measure your water into a heat-safe container, then add the lye.

Step 2: Mix the lye into the water until fully dissolved. Set aside to cool until it reaches room temperature.

Step 3: While this is cooling, melt the coconut oil in a microwave-safe container.

Step 4: When the lye water and the coconut oil are at room temperature, combine them in a heat-safe container. Whisk them together until fully combined.

Step 5: Mix in the sea salt, then pour into your containers. Let it cool completely before covering with your soap tops.

Wine Soap

Wine is a great ingredient for soap. It adds a lot of beneficial antioxidants and vitamins to your soap.

Ingredients:

Water – 4 ounces (113 grams)
Lye – 1.5 ounces (42 grams)
Coconut Oil – 0.5 ounces (14 grams)
Red Wine – 2 ounces (57 grams)
Dried or Fresh Rosemary Leaves – 1 tablespoon (4 grams)

Instructions:

Step 1: Measure your water into a heat-safe container, then add the lye. Mix the lye into the water until fully dissolved. Set aside to cool until it reaches room temperature.

Step 2: While this is cooling, melt the coconut oil in a microwave-safe container.

Step 3: Combine the coconut oil with the red wine, and stir until completely blended.

Step 4: Once the lye-water has reached room temperature, slowly pour it into the wine-coconut oil mixture, stirring constantly.

Step 5: Add your rosemary leaves to the soap mixture, and stir well.

Step 6: Pour the soap into your mold of choice (silicone molds are recommended), and allow to cool for 24 hours.

Grapefruit Soap

Grapefruit is another great ingredient to add to soap. It helps your skin heal faster, and it has a very refreshing scent.

Ingredients:

Water – 4 ounces (113 grams)
Lye – 1.5 ounces (42 grams)
Coconut Oil – .5 ounces (14 grams)
Olive Oil – .5 ounces (14 grams)
Grapefruit Essential Oil – 6 drops

Instructions:

Step 1: Measure your water, and put it in a pot.

Step 2: Put your lye into the pot of water, and stir until it has dissolved. Make sure you are wearing gloves and eye protection. This is a very corrosive chemical, so you don't want to get it on your skin or in your eyes. Also, be careful not to breathe in any fumes that come off of the chemical when it dissolves.

Step 3: After the lye is dissolved, remove the pot from the heat and let it cool for about 5 minutes. Then add your coconut oil, olive oil, and Grapefruit Essential Oil. (The Grapefruit Essential Oil will help with healing skin faster.) Don't try to cool down too much because this soap will trace quickly! Trace happens when all of the soap has turned into a thick liquid instead of a thick paste. If you have a high-melting-point oil (like coconut), don't use olive oil because the two won't mix very well together if they're too cold – they'll separate when they're poured into the mold!

Step 4: Pour your soap into your mold while it's still liquid. Since this recipe contains fast-moving ingredients like coconut oil, you have to work fast.

Step 5: After your soap has cooled, cut it into bars using a soap cutter.

Cedarwood Soap

Cedarwood is a wonderful scent made popular by men's cologne. It has a warm and woodsy smell.

Ingredients:

Water – 4 ounces (113 grams)
Lye – 1.5 ounces (42 grams)
Coconut Oil – .5 ounces (14 grams)
Castor Oil – .5 ounces (14 grams)
Cedarwood Essential Oil – 1.5 grams
Melted Beeswax – 1.5 ounces (42 grams)

Instructions:

Step 1: Measure out your water. Add the lye to the water and stir gently until dissolved.

Step 2: Weigh out your coconut oil, castor oil, and beeswax. Put the oil and wax into a glass measuring cup.

Step 3: Add the lye water to the cup with your oils and wax. Stir gently at first until the oils are completely melted, then stir vigorously for 30 seconds. This will allow some of the water to evaporate off. It also helps incorporate air into the soap, which allows it to set up faster.

Step 4: Pour into molds and let cool for 24 hours. Unmold and cut into bars. Let cure for 4 weeks before using or giving as gifts!

Cinnamon Soap

This is a common kitchen spice used in many cooking recipes. This is not to be confused with cassia (a different kind of cinnamon). Cinnamon has a sweet smell that makes it perfect for the holidays!

Ingredients:

Water – 4 ounces (113 grams)
Cinnamon Oil – 0.28 ounce (8 grams)
Lye Water – 4 ounces (113 grams)
Olive Oil or Sunflower Oil – 1 ounce (30 grams)

Instructions:

Step 1: Place water in a saucepan and bring it to a boil. Watch carefully so it does not boil over. Turn off the heat. Add lye to the water and stir until dissolved. Let cool for several minutes. Add oil and stir well.

Step 2: Once the soap is at 110 °F (43 °C), place in a mold and pour the lye solution over it slowly in a thin stream while stirring with a stick blender or hand beater; continue stirring for about 5 minutes (mixture will be thick).

Step 3: Let it sit undisturbed for 1 hour. Cover with a lid or plastic wrap and let sit overnight. Remove soap from mold, cut in bars, and allow to cure for 4 – 6 weeks before use. This gives the soap time to harden and the cinnamon scent time to develop. If you can wait that long! Enjoy!

Chocolate Soap

Like many other soaps, this smells great! Who doesn't like the smell of chocolate?

Ingredients:

Water – 4 ounces (113 grams)
Cocoa Butter – 1 ounce (28 grams)
Lye Water – 5 ounces (142 grams)
Lard or Coconut Oil – 1.2 ounces (34 grams)

Instructions:

Step 1: Gather all of your ingredients together, and place them in a heat-safe container. When you are ready to make your soap, make sure that all of the ingredients are at room temperature.

Step 2: Slowly add the lye water to the heated oils and butter. Be very careful during this step; do not breathe in any fumes that may escape from the container.

Step 3: Stir until everything is mixed in, and then add your fragrance oil or essential oil at this time as well.

Step 4: Pour into molds and allow to cool for 24 hours before removing from the mold. Allow bars to cure for 4-6 weeks before using them; this will help remove any excess moisture that remains in the bars.

Champagne Soap

This is a very feminine scent that smells just like the real thing!

Ingredients:

Water – 4 ounces (113 grams)
Lard or Coconut Oil – 1.2 ounces (34 grams)
Lye Water – 5 ounces (142 grams)
Champagne Fragrance Oil – 3 drops/0.1 ounces (3 grams)

Instructions:

Step 1: Measure out the water, lard, and lye into a heat-safe container.

Step 2: Stir constantly until the lye is completely dissolved.

Step 3: Cover and let sit overnight.

Step 4: The next day, uncover and add the Champagne Fragrance Oil and stir well.

Step 5: Pour into molds. I used an ice cube tray with each cube being 1 ounce of soap.

Step 6: Let sit for 24 hours to harden, unmold and cut into bars.

Rosemary Soap

Rosemary is a great herb that can be used for many things. It also has a very strong scent that helps keep those pesky bugs away naturally.

Ingredients:

Water – 4 ounces (113 grams)
Coconut oil – 1 ounce (28 grams)
Castor oil – 2 ounces (56 grams)
Lye (sodium hydroxide) – 4 teaspoons (20 grams)
Lemon essential oil – 5 drops
Rosemary essential oil – 5 drops

Instructions:

Step 1: Combine the lye and water in a heat-safe container. Stir until all of the lye is dissolved. Set aside to cool.

Step 2: In a separate container, combine the coconut oil, castor oil, and rosemary essential oil. Melt together over low heat until melted and well blended.

Step 3: When both mixtures are at room temperature, pour the oils into the lye water and stir slowly and carefully until combined.

Step 4: Pour the mixture into your soap mold(s). Cover with a layer of plastic wrap or parchment paper and let sit for 24 hours to harden.

Step 5: Remove from the mold after 24 hours and cut into bars as desired. Let dry for at least 48 hours so that it can harden completely and remove moisture before using.

Strawberry Soap

Strawberry is a popular fruit that has many uses. It is delicious and can be used in a variety of recipes. It can also provide a sweet scent to your homemade soaps.

Ingredients:

Water – 4 ounces (113 grams)
Lye – 4 ounces (113 grams)
Strawberry fragrance oil (optional) – 4 ounces (113 grams)
Glycerin (or vegetable glycerin) – 5 ounces (140 grams)
Water – 5 ounces (140 grams)
Mango Butter – 1 ounce (28 grams)

2% super fat

Instructions:

Step 1: Measure and melt the soap base on low heat in a microwave-safe container.

Step 2: Measure and dissolve lye into 4 ounces (113 grams) of water. Allow cooling to 150 degrees F (65 degrees C).

Step 3: Slowly add the lye solution into the melted soap base, stirring slowly.

Step 4: Add a few drops of strawberry fragrance oil.

Step 5: Allow the mixture to cool until it becomes thick, then pour it into your prepared mold(s).

Step 6: Allow the soap to fully harden overnight before unmolding and wrapping it in plastic wrap or cellophane for storage.

Vanilla Extract Soap

Vanilla extract is an organic product made from vanilla beans that are infused in a liquid and allowed to sit for at least six months. The fragrant aroma of vanilla makes it a great addition to homemade soaps.

Ingredients:

Water – 4 ounces (113 grams)
Lye – 4 ounces (113 grams)
Vanilla Extract – 2 ounces (56 grams)
Olive Oil – 4 ounces (113 grams)

Instructions:

Step 1: Gather all the ingredients and equipment. Set up your lye container, mixing bowl, stick blender, and soap mold.

Step 2: Weigh out the water and pour it into the mixing bowl. Weigh out the lye and slowly add to the water (lye is caustic and you don't want to splash it on your skin or eyes). Stir with a plastic or wooden spoon for about five minutes until it turns clear.

Step 3: Add the olive oil and stir until well blended. Add the vanilla extract and stir until well blended.

Step 4: Pour into prepared molds and allow to sit for 24 hours. Remove from the mold (if desired), cut into bars, wrap in tissue paper then store in an airtight container until ready to use.

Chapter 4: Tips and Tricks

In this chapter, you will learn some tips and tricks that will help you a lot in your soap-making journey.

How to use an existing recipe, and modify it

One of the best ways to learn is by experience. Look for a recipe that you'd like to try, and follow it exactly as written. If you don't intend to make the soap right away, write down everything you did from start to finish. Take notes and study them later while trying to figure out what went wrong (if anything), or right!

When you have the recipe perfected, tweak it however you like. If it calls for too much of an ingredient, use then less. If there isn't enough of something, put in more. But try not to stray too far from the original recipe, unless you're making a completely different kind of soap with a different purpose in mind.

Keep in mind that some oils are easier to work with than others. Using oils that are easy to work with will make your job much easier than using difficult oils (which is one reason why I recommend olive oil).

Some oils will harden up your soap too much or make it too soft – so if your original recipe only calls for 1-part coconut oil and 1-part olive oil, but your mixture turns out way too soft or hard when you use this ratio of coconut and olive oil, then you need to adjust your recipe. You can use more coconut oil, or less olive oil until the desired consistency is reached.

Or (if your recipe is a good one), you can try using a different kind of oil altogether. For example, if you're using an olive oil soap recipe that turns out too soft and thin when you use the called for a mix of olive and coconut oils, then replace the part of the olive oil with some palm kernel or babassu oil instead – this will thicken up your soap a bit (but it won't make it feel oily).

How to make a recipe from scratch?

When you're starting from scratch, you can use any recipe as a guideline. But always remember that the finished product will be different when you make a soap recipe from scratch than when you start with a premade recipe (because your soap base will be different). This is why writing down everything you do is so important – so you can remember how much of each ingredient to add when making a new batch.

For every 100 grams of base oil:

10 grams of fragrance or essential oils (if using)

5 grams of Vitamin E or other preservatives (if using)

If you're using lye without an added preservative, then add 1 gram of lye per 30 grams of base oils. So if your base oil total is 100 grams, then your lye total will be about 3 grams. If your base oil total is 210 grams, then your lye total will be about 6 grams. If your base oil total is 300 grams, then your lye total will be about 9 grams. And so on…

1 gram of stearic acid per 40 kilos of oils if desired (can also use 10% super fatting agent instead) Note: The stearic acid is added to help with the hardness of your soap.

10 grams of sodium hydroxide per 100 grams of base oils (or 3% super fatting agent if desired)

If you're making a bar of solid soap, then add 1% of bentonite clay per kilo of oils.

If you're making liquid soap, then add 3% of glycerin per kilo of oils.

For a soft oily bar soap that will lather easily, add 0.5% sodium lactate per kilo of oils. (This is optional – but it helps the lather.)

You can use the above guidelines to create whatever type of soap you like (liquid soap, bar soap, creamy soap, etc.), as long as you keep the ratios of each ingredient consistent. This is why writing down everything you do is so important – so you can make these changes later if needed!

Understanding the science behind soap making

Soap making is a science, but don't let that intimidate you. Start with a simple recipe and you'll see that it's not as hard as you might think!

Soap is made with oils and lye, and it's saponified when the lye combines with the oil. When the soap is finished, it's called "lye soap." After the saponification process, your lye soap will contain a high percentage of glycerin (which helps moisturize your skin).

You might be asking yourself why glycerin is important – well, it has to do with the science of soap making. Soap making works because of an ionic reaction between oils and lye water. The main component in oils is fatty acids, while lye water consists of alkaline hydroxides (also known as bases). The reaction between fatty acids and alkaline hydroxides forms soap and glycerin (and other byproducts). The fattier acids there are in your oils combined with the number of alkaline hydroxides in your lye water equals how much glycerin you end up having in your finished product.

How to mix colors

When it comes to creating colored soaps, you can use any color you like. You can mix different colors too! You can create pastels, bright colors, and even metallic – it's up to your creative imagination.

If you're mixing colors, and you have kids or pets at home, make sure the soap is in a contained area that's impossible for them to reach. If a spill occurs, make sure to clean it up immediately (with an absorbent pad) before the soap hardens up again.

Different color pigments require different amounts of soap. If you want to use an entire bar of soap to make a colored batch, you'll need more soap than if you wanted to make just a few bars. If you're using a pre-made soap as the base, then you might need less soap than if you were to use an entire bar.

If you don't want to mix colors yourself, then there are many colored soap bases available. These bases do require a lot of soap (usually at least one full bar). If you go this route, it's good to make sure that whatever colored soap base you decide on is food grade and safe for your skin.

To mix colors with a premade base:

You can choose to mix the colors in a separate bowl (with water), or you can add small amounts of each color directly into the batch that contains the pre-made colored base. Depending on how many color you want in your final product, will determine how much powder to use for each color. I recommend adding just a little at a time so that it's easier to control how much additional color goes into your batch. You can always add more later if needed.

If you choose to add colors directly into the premade-colored base, make sure to mix well. You don't want undissolved color chunks in your final product.

To get a pastel or light color, start with a small amount of color at a time, and add more as needed. If you start with too much color right away, you can end up with a dark color – which may not be what you intended. You can always add more later if needed.

When using an undiluted colored soap base:

These bases are usually made using only one single color – and they tend to be quite concentrated when it comes to the amount of soap that's included in each bar. This means that these bases require very little additional soap (if any) to get the desired mix of colors for your final product – but this is also why these bases often cost more than premade colored soaps that contain multiple colors already blended. These types of bases are best used as is, and only require adding water (if desired). Simply melt down the entire bar before adding your additional ingredients (essential oils or herbs). I recommend adding 1-part colored base to 2-parts water if any additional water is added at all.

Tips for using colorants

When you're using powdered colorants, be sure to mix them into the soap very well. I like to use a whisk or electric mixer for this. If you don't mix the colorant well enough, you could end up with undissolved chunks of color in your final product.

Distilled water is best when it comes to coloring your soap. Tap water can sometimes leave a residue on the surface of your soap that makes the color appear dull and less vibrant. Distilled water also helps to keep minerals from forming inside your soap molds if there happens to be some leftover after rinsing them out.

When it comes to adding additional water, I recommend using distilled water only – usually about 1-part colored base to 2-parts distilled water is sufficient (for most colored bases). The amount of additional water will vary depending on what you're using as a base for coloring – how concentrated it is, how many colors you need, etc.

How to make your colorants:

When it comes to making your colorants, there are many different ways you can do this. You can use dye powders, micas (which are minerals), mica chips (which add shimmer), clay chips or powders, herbs of all kinds, spices (such as cinnamon), flower petals – the list is endless. I'm going to focus on the easiest and most cost-effective way to make your colorants using herbs and spices.

To make colorants using herbs:

Some popular herbs you can use for making colorant are Dandelion Leaf, Red Clover, Licorice Root (which also adds a nice scent), Mullein, Chamomile, and Calendula flowers. You can use either the dried or freshly picked herb. If you're using fresh flowers, blanch them in boiling water for about 30 seconds to a minute before using them in your soap-making projects. You can also freeze fresh flowers – just make sure they are totally dry when you store them in the freezer. The color will become more vibrant once your soap is ready! It's best to use whole dried herbs when mixing colors. If you have leftover bits of fragrant herbs in your soap batch, it will add a nice scent too! You can also add dried flower buds of any type (such as lavender buds) to add some extra color and scent – but the fragrance won't come out as strong as it would if added directly to the soap base or melted down.

To make colorants using spices:

Many different spices can be used to make colorants. Some ideas for common herbs/spices you can use for creating colorants include Turmeric (which will add a yellow hue), Paprika, Cloves, Cinnamon, Vanilla Beans (which will add a brown hue), and Black Tea (which will add a bright red or pink hue). You can use whole dried spices or grind them up before adding them to your soap batch. Whole dried spices are best used when mixing different colors. It's best to use ground-up spices when adding color directly into the premade-colored base (if using).

If you don't want all the spice in your soap, then you should grind it up into powder before adding it to your soap base. Make sure there are no large chunks or clumps of spice left in your soap base.

If you want to make a colorant using spices, then it's best to create a separate batch of soap and add the desired colorants into the batch once it's finished (while the soap is still soft). If you want to add spices directly into the premade-colored base (if using), then grind them up first. It's best to use whole dried spices for this method – but ground-up spices can work too. I recommend grinding up whichever spices you choose to use into a fine powder before adding them to your soap base. This will ensure there are no large chunks or clumps of spice left in your soap base.

How to make swirls or other patterns in the soap?

Swirls are a great way to add some extra interest to your soaps. You can make swirls by hand or with a tool (we'll talk about tools in the next section).

To make swirls by hand, you'll need a long, narrow spatula. Dip the spatula into one color of the soap. Then, swirl it around on top of the soap until you get the pattern you want. It's better to do this quickly so that the soap doesn't harden. If you happen to smear it everywhere, then it's okay! You can just scoop up some more soap and try again.

If you want more precise swirls, then it would be best to use an old toothbrush or a silicone piping bag with a tip (to help control where the soap is placed). While these tools do help in creating more precise designs and patterns, they do take longer than using your hands. But they also give you more precision in design – especially if you aren't completely confident with making swirls by hand.

How to make swirls or other patterns with a special tool

If you want to add some extra interest to your soaps, then you can use a special tool to add designs and patterns. These tools are called soap funnels (or sometimes hand pipes). There are many different styles and sizes of funnels out there, but the basic idea is the same for all of them. They're a pipe that you can pour the soap into and out of. Some even have a cap on one end so that it's easier to pour and less messy.

To use the funnel, start by melting your base in a microwave-safe container (or double boiler). Then, scoop some soap into the funnel and let it harden for about 30 seconds before pouring it into the mold. Make sure that you don't pour too much at once! If you do, then it might come out unevenly or leave gaps in your design. You want just enough soap in the funnel to make sure that it will fill up the entire mold with no gaps or empty spots left behind. If you overfill it, then just add more melted soap later until your design is filled out.

You can also use piping bags and tips (similar to what we talked about earlier). You'll want to make sure that the tip is small enough to fit through your soap mold. If it's too big, then you may need to cut the end off or heat the tip so that you can shape it a bit (depending on the mold). Then, just squeeze some soap into the mold. Make sure that you don't put too much, though! Otherwise, it will be harder to clean up or leave gaps in your design.

How to add special effects such as glitter

Gemstones are also a great way to add special effects to your soap. You can either buy them pre-made, or you can create your own.

To create your gemstones, you'll need to melt a small batch of colored soap (just enough to cover the bottom of your pan), pour it into a shallow container, and sprinkle the glitter over top. Leave it for a few minutes so that the glitter can stick to the soap. Then, scoop the soaps out and let them cool.

You can also purchase powdered pigments which are used in art projects to add colors and other effects to glass and ceramics. These pigments are made with metal oxides – they contain no dyes or pigments (even if they're labeled "pigment"). They also come in many different colors.

When using powdered pigments, make sure that you use colors that are safe for skin contact. Don't inhale the powder too much while working with them either!

If you want larger glitters in your soap, then you might want to use clear glycerin soap instead of opaque soap bases. If you do use glycerin soap, make sure that it is food grade – otherwise, it could end up discoloring your soap.

Conclusion

Making soap is a fun hobby, and when you are done you will have some beautiful bars of artfully made soap to show off or give as gifts. You can even start your line of unique and desirable products. Soap making is a fun hobby that can be enjoyed by anyone with the desire to try their hand at something new.

"If you love what you do, you'll never work a day in your life". Soap making is one such activity where you can enjoy yourself and relax while making these useful and beautiful products.

Do remember that these recipes are given as a guideline only. You can make variations of these recipes to suit your specific needs. There are many books written on the subject, so you can find many more tips and tricks for making soap!

Now that you know how to make soap, you can go forth and try out all the different recipes and come up with your own. Have fun with it!

Manufactured by Amazon.ca
Bolton, ON

27123420R00044